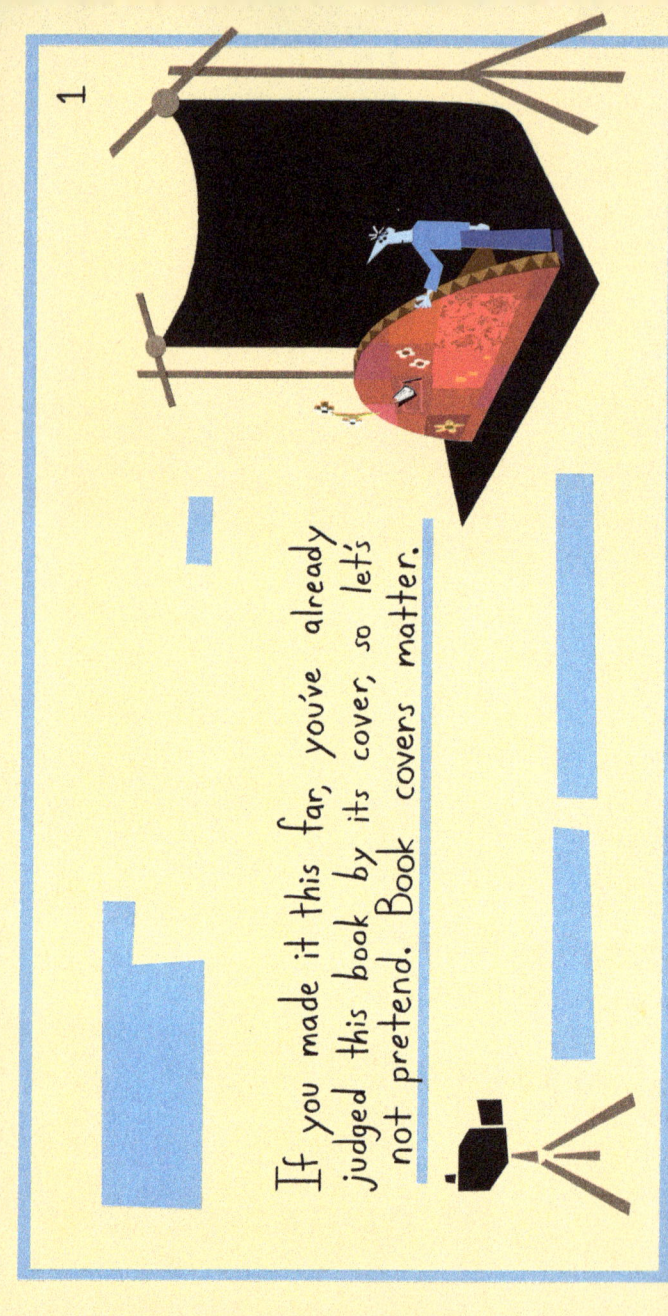

REALITY CHECK DEFINED...

Definition of *reality check* : something that clarifies or serves as a reminder of reality often by correcting a misconception. Merriam Webster Online (https://www.merriam-webster.com/dictionary/reality-%20check).

How often have you encountered a statement that you wished were true but couldn't be entirely sure it was? Even though most people might seem to agree that the statement was true, you still had your doubts. Perhaps you didn't want to appear to be ignorant, or feel fearful, negative or unconfident (pick your own adjective), so you just blindly assumed that everybody else knew something you didn't know and accepted that at face value. Here are a couple examples: Maybe you spent lots of money and time on a poor business choice because you wanted to believe you can do anything you set your mind to. Or maybe you stayed in the wrong relationship for too long because you wanted to believe love will conquer all. Sound familiar? Then read on.

In my own journey, I've been fortunate to develop a successful business as an attorney with a solo practice. Attorneys want evidence. When something is presented to me, it's my job to ask: Is that actually true? Answering that question usually leads to better decisions— for my clients and for me — because those decisions derive from critical thinking and personal truths.

This book does not presume there is only one truth or reality. It does, however, acknowledge that too many people spend too much time deceiving themselves and others, often unintentionally. Somewhere inside each of us is a compass that tells us what is true and real. Life can be simpler when we get in touch with that compass. Consequently, this book is designed to help you develop the habit of questioning the amount of truth invested in things you're told and subsequently pass on to others. My hope is that developing that habit will empower you to address life's complexities more effectively.

To jumpstart the process of creating your own reality checks, this book includes a set of alternatives to many popular assumptions and sayings, including maxims, axioms, proverbs, quotes, prevailing assumptions and the like. The point of the following reality checks is that you need not pretend anything said or assumed is true just because it sounds or feels good. If you develop the habit of finding your own reality checks, your mental health will flourish.

NEGATIVITY

AND

POSITIVITY

We constantly confront supposedly *inspirational* advice telling us to strive to always be positive, no matter the circumstance. Why? Feelings of negativity, anxiety or fear are not automatically bad. Sometimes, allegedly *bad* feelings arise for *good* reasons. We should learn to cope with them without guilt.

Experience may be a better goal than happiness.

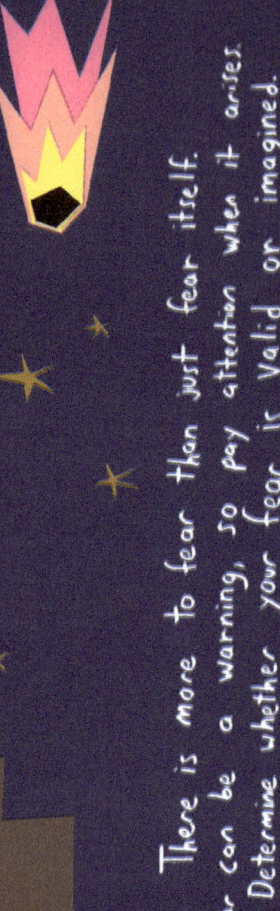

There is more to fear than just fear itself. Fear can be a warning, so pay attention when it arises. Determine whether your fear is valid or imagined.

It's trite to say, be happy or be positive. Instead, when inevitable times of sadness or negativity crop up, look for comfort in the fact that no feeling is permanent.

Sometimes, you cannot avoid sweating the small stuff. When the small stuff causes too much perspiration, look for as many distractions as possible.

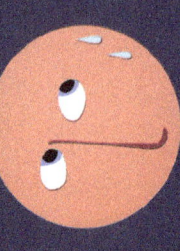

We hear many platitudes about what it takes to be successful. Too many of them suggest that you can achieve any success with enough determination, but that's unrealistic. Maybe so. Maybe not. Most paths to success require objective thinking about how to achieve your goals.

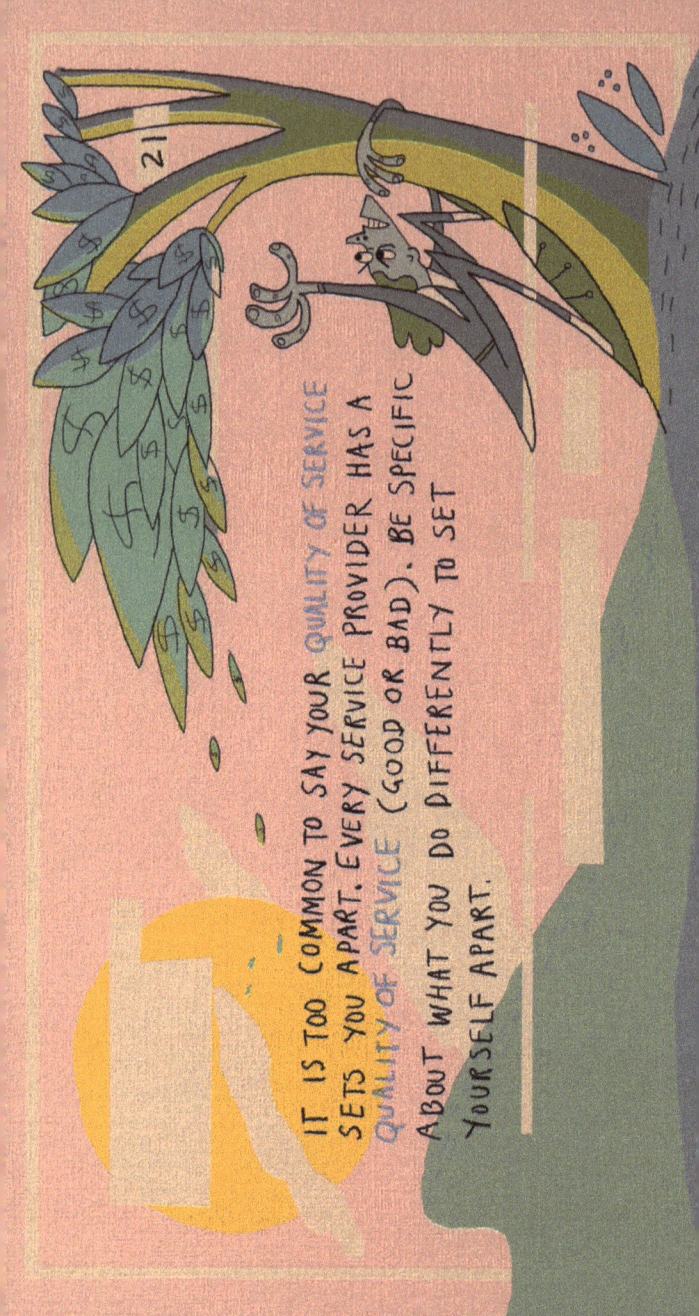

Too much of what is said about love is overly romanticized. Love and relationships require time, effort, dialog, compromise and critical thinking — just like other aspects of our lives.

It may be better to go to bed angry than it would be to stay up and try to resolve an argument when you're tired and not thinking straight.

Love does not conquer all. Many well-loved people have died horrible deaths alone after months or years of suffering.

There are no perfect people, so there is no perfect person for you. But there may be many excellent people for you.

Opposites may attract, but they can fight frequently. For a peaceful, long-term relationship, find someone with similar interests.

Self-denial seems to be a common theme when it comes to your health. Why do so many people pretend that it's easy to stay fit and healthy? Good health is a worthy goal that deserves to be discussed with complete honesty.

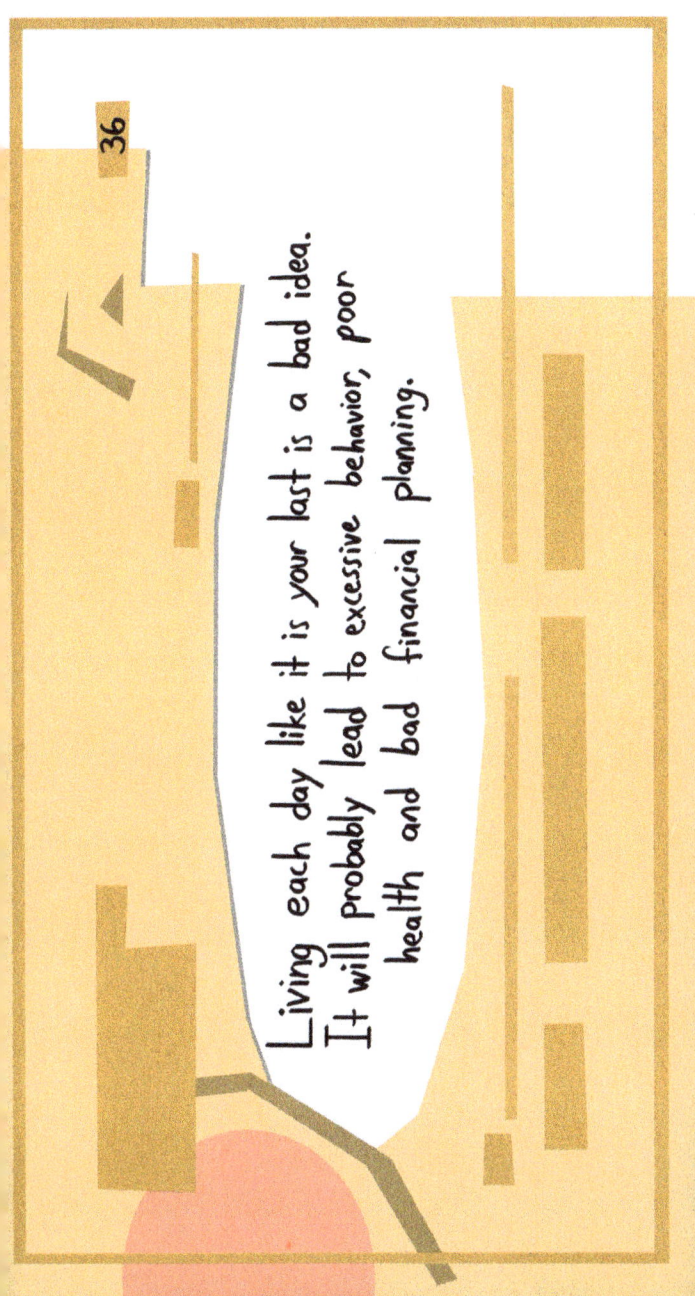

For most people, discipline frequently gives way to lack of discipline. Strive for consistent moderation to acheive good health.

38

Any advice that guaranties you will change your health by eliminating or adding one particular item to your diet is probably bad advice.

Unhealthy desserts with refined carbohydrates taste better than fresh fruit. Don't try to say otherwise.

If someone is in denial, advising him that his weight is unhealthy for his height and age is not body shaming.

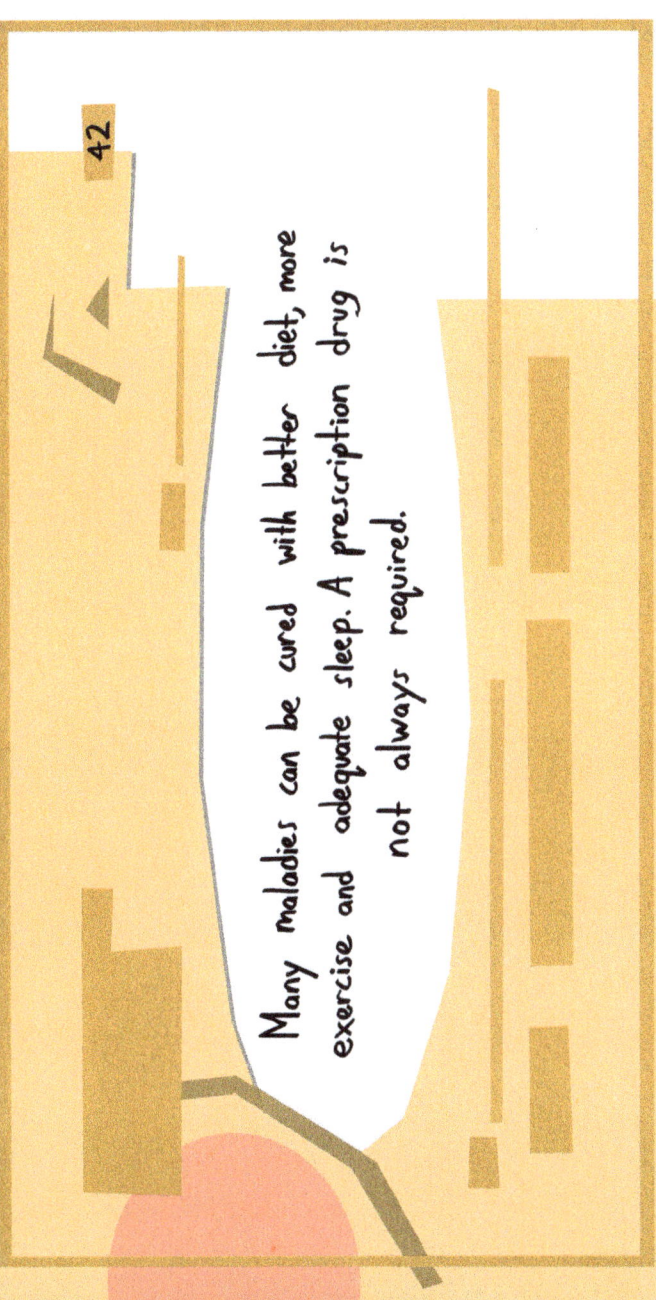

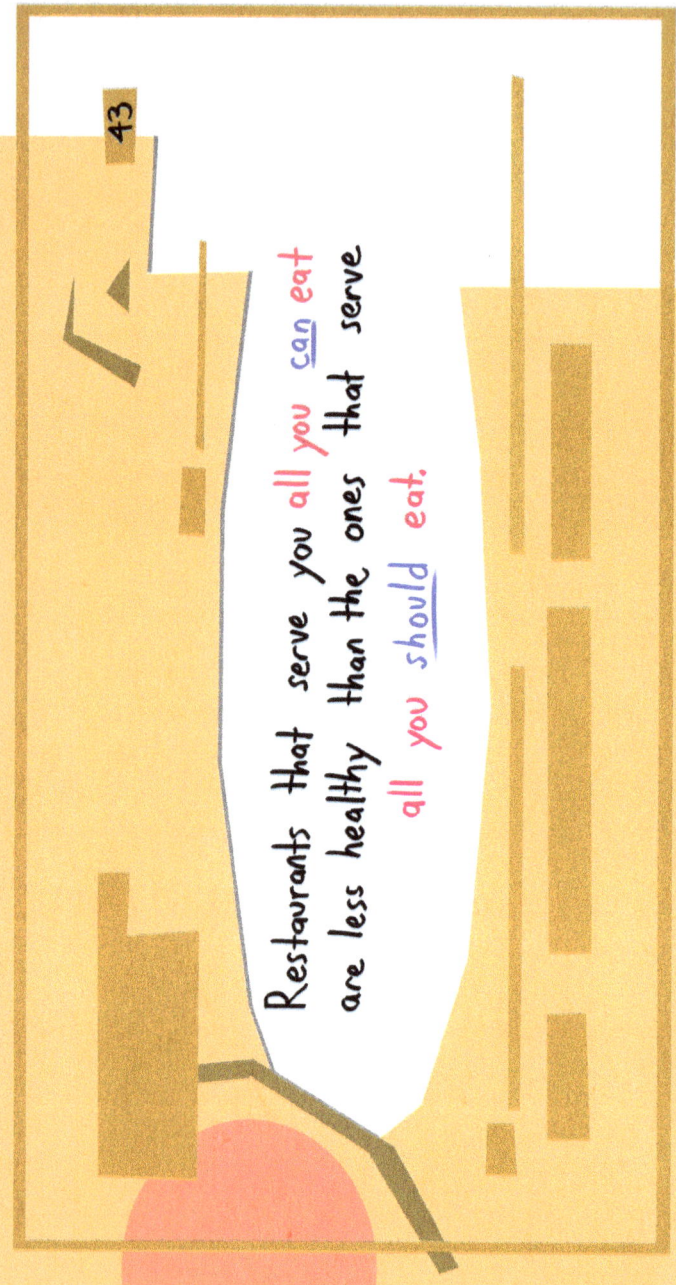

THE THINGS PEOPLE SAY ABOUT BEAUTY CAN BE ANNOYINGLY PANDERING AND CONTRADICTORY. FOR EXAMPLE, THE SAME MAGAZINES THAT DISPLAY COVERS WITH IMPOSSIBLY BEAUTIFUL PEOPLE INCLUDE ARTICLES ABOUT HOW TRUE BEAUTY COMES FROM WITHIN. THE FOLLOWING REALITY CHECKS ATTEMPT TO INJECT SOME AUTHENTICITY INTO THE DISCUSSION OF BEAUTY.

WITH FEW EXCEPTIONS, ONE'S PHYSICAL BEAUTY IS USUALLY ASSOCIATED WITH YOUTH. AS YOU AGE, PRIORITIZE OTHER BEAUTIFUL QUALITIES LIKE WISDOM, EXPERIENCE AND PERSPECTIVE.

MOVIE STARS AND MODELS FREQUENTLY SAY THAT THEY LOOKED HORRIBLE OR NERDY WHEN THEY WERE YOUNGER, BUT IT'S PROBABLY NOT TRUE. MANY OF THEM HAVE LOOKED FANTASTIC SINCE BIRTH.

PARENTING and CHILDREN

People love to give advice about raising children, yet that advice ignores that each parent and child is unique. Many adults also seem to assume that they deserve more respect than children, even though we're all just people, no matter what our age. The following reality checks attempt to correct those misconceptions.

Children should not be told to automatically respect their parents, elders or anyone else. This concept allows for abuse. A child's respect should be earned.

Having a great kid does not make you an expert. You may just be lucky. Be humble and sparing with your parenting advice.

It doesn't take a village to raise your children if you live in a sucky village. Do what you can to move to a better neighborhood.

Parents influence their children but cannot be responsible for all their good or bad qualities. You are not your parents.

RESOLVING PROBLEMS

My experience as an attorney has taught me that no single systemized approach will resolve all problems. Still, I have found that the path to a good solution usually involves some combination of listening, observing and being flexible. The reality checks below summarize some of the lessons I've learned.

Being realistic about what's possible and what's not can help resolve conflict.

A threat should be a promise in negotiations. Following through on a threat can make your adversary trust you, which can lead to resolution.

The notion that you or others will get what they deserve—positively or negatively—does not always pan out. Base your actions on what you believe is right.

Better education doesn't always make for better people. Sometimes, better education just helps blowhards and users to acheive their goals.

No doubt, some teams can accomplish incredible results, but reality checks below consider the power and importance of the individual.

Saying there is no I in team merely demonstrates you know how to spell. Great teams can, and probably should, include members with unique approaches and perspectives.

If you don't like working in a team, find situations in which you can work alone.

If everyone felt the same about faith, the world would need only one religion. When you encounter a statement that elevates one belief system over another, pause and consider whether that messaging is valid.

We search for truth, yet it's hard to find. The following reality checks seek to sniff out falsehoods and insincerities.

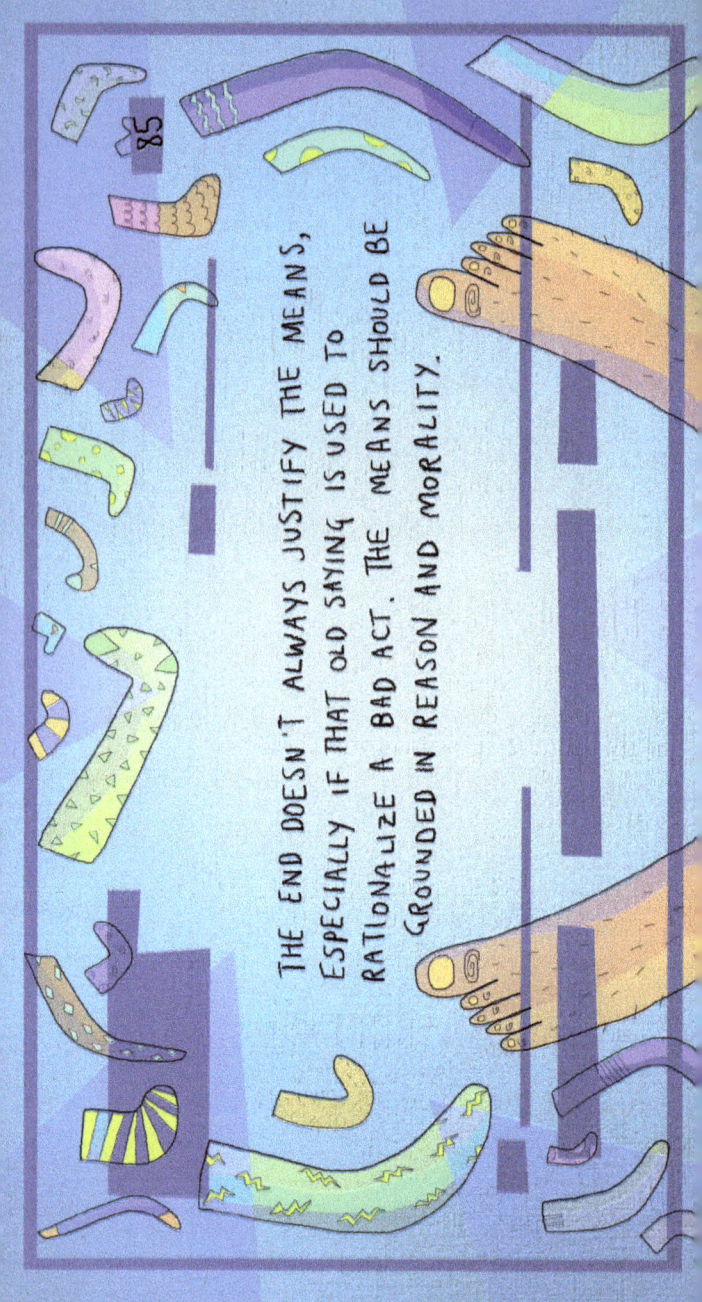

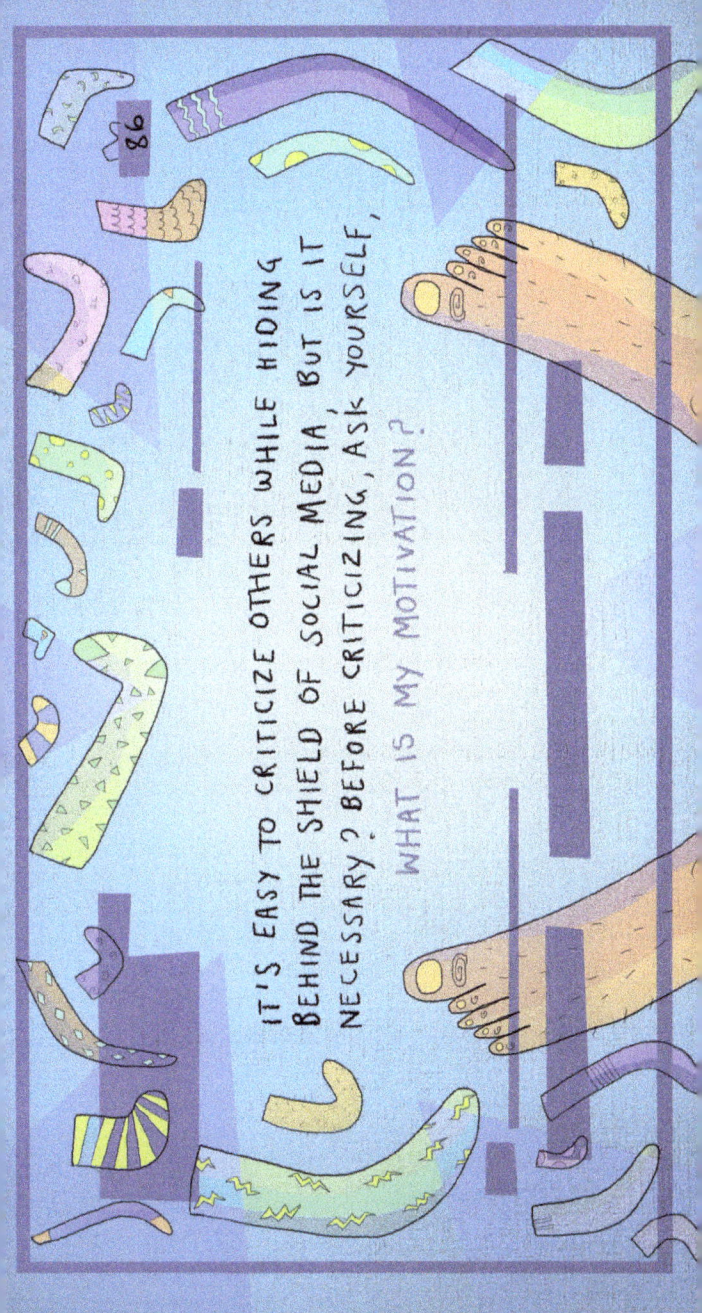

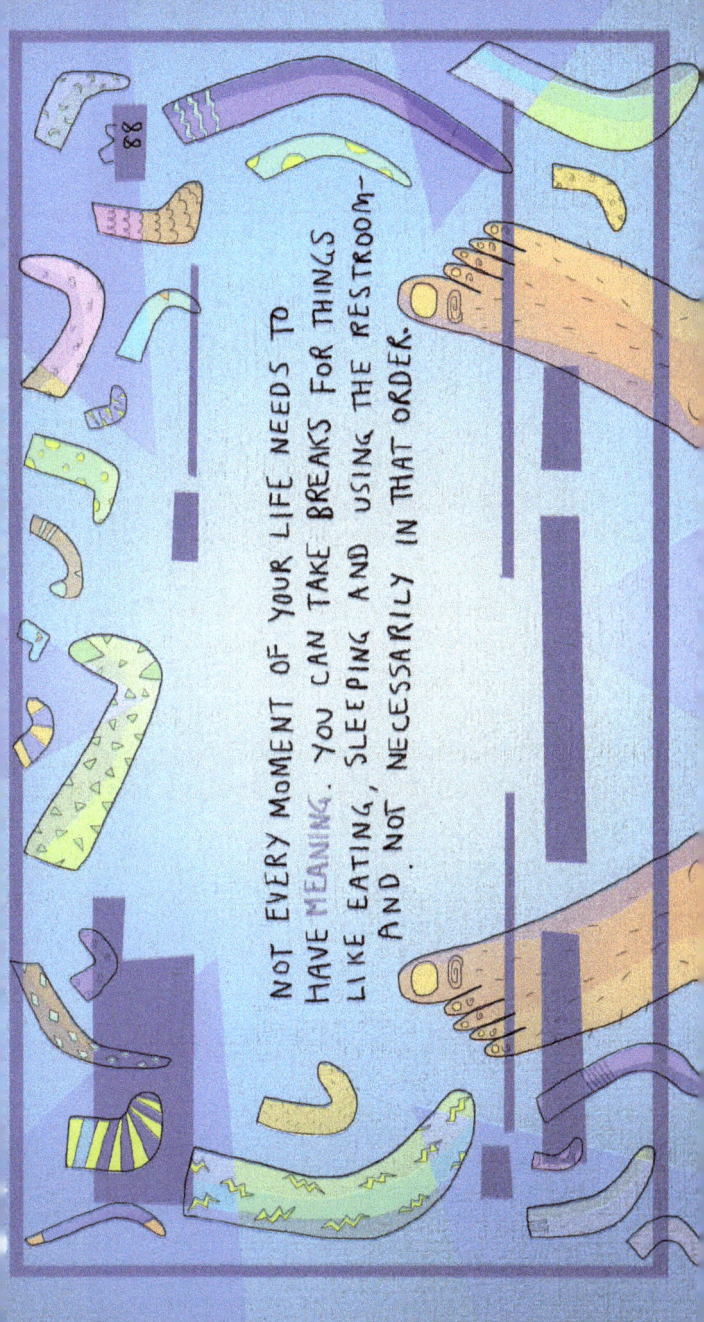

Quality is usually superior to quantity. Yet, we are barraged with quantity in many facets of life. The Internet drowns us in information.

Movies are longer. Drinks and meals are supersized. Why? Less deserves more consideration. That's why this book is short.

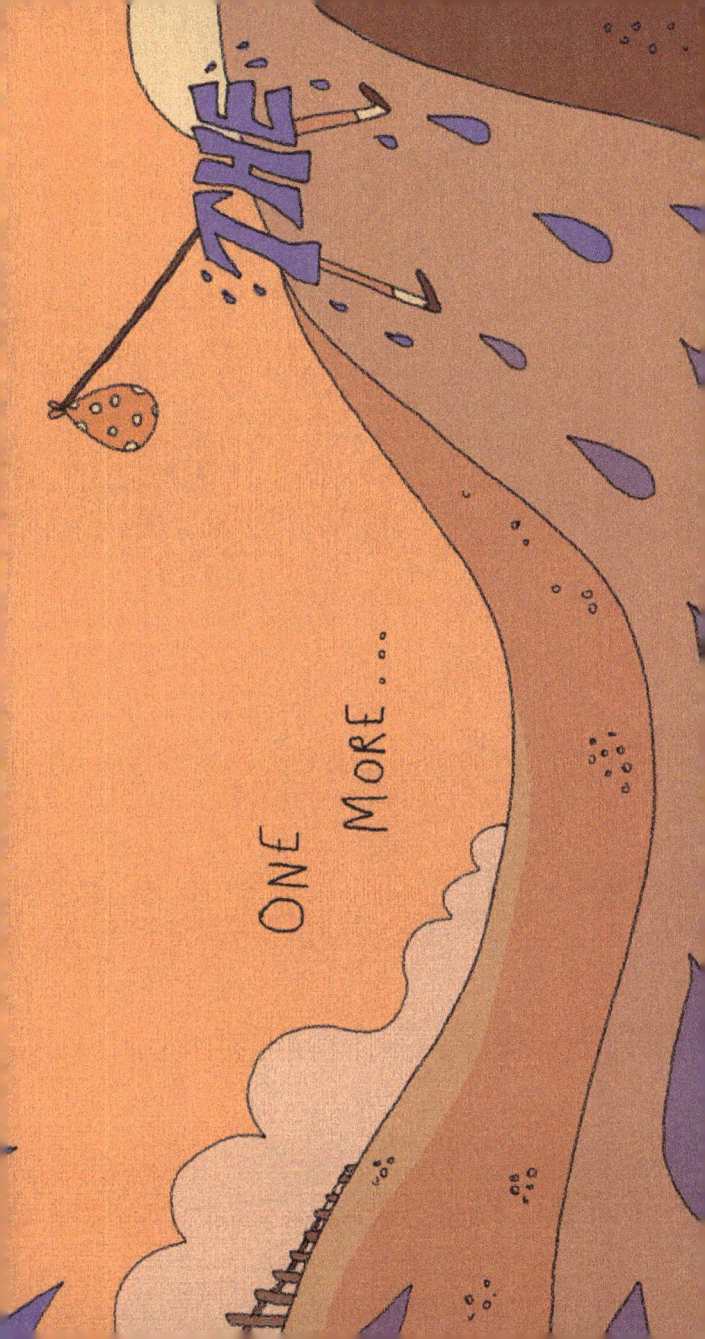

THE IS THERE TO FILL SPACE. IF WE ELIMINATED THE FROM THE ENGLISH LANGUAGE, WE COULD USE FEWER WORDS.

DISCLAIMER:

In an imperfect attempt to be gender neutral, this book alternates between *he* and *she*.

ABOUT THE AUTHOR

David E. Libman, Esq., LL.M. resides in Southern California with his wife of 21 years, Andrea Carel-Libman. Their two boys (now, young adults), Mathieu and Joel, are in college. David feels very lucky to have such an incredible family, but he's done other things in his life, too. A graduate of the Juilliard School, David worked as a professional drummer for years before changing careers to law. Now in his seventeenth year as an attorney, David focuses his solo practice on solution-finding in the arenas of business, real estate and estate planning. David's many publications include: multiple legal articles for the Orange County Lawyer Magazine, Chapman Law Review, and the M&A Tax Report; musical articles and product reviews for DRUM!Magazine; and an instructional book published by Mel Bay, entitled The Essential Drumset Method. David frequently gives speeches and is available to do so regarding his 100 Reality Checks.

SPECIAL THANKS

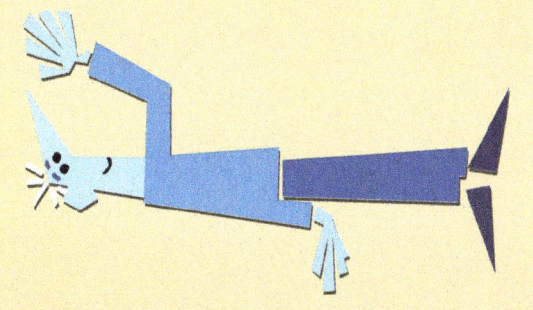

THANK YOU TO:

My wife Andrea for sharing your life with me, and for your love, support, inspiration, constant dialog and companionship.

Our boys Mathieu and Joel for being such fantastic people. You make me very proud, and I love you both very much.

Andy Doerschuk for being such a great editor on this book and in general, and for making me realize this is not a book of quotes.

Mathieu Libman, Sam Lane and Bryan Lee for their incredible artwork for this book.

Laura Sala, Steve Smith, Marcin Spatzier, Jim Haley and Lance LaBelle for their willingness to read drafts of this book and offer thoughtful comments.

www.ingramcontent.com/pod-product-compliance
Lightning Source LLC
Chambersburg PA
CBHW061232070526
44584CB00030B/4086